tea
& infusions

To all my tea-drinking friends around the world

RIGHT

**POSTER BY GEORGES
DE FLEURE.**

OPPOSITE

**A FORTUNE-TELLING
DEVICE.**

PAGE 4

**(TOP LEFT) EAST INDIA
WHARF, 1756; (TOP
RIGHT)** *CAMELLIA THEA;*
**(BELOW) AZERBAIJANI
TEA DIRECTORS.**

PAGE 5

**(TOP LEFT) AFTERNOON
TEA; (TOP RIGHT) TEA-
STEAMED FISH; (BELOW
LEFT) FRUIT INFUSIONS;
(BELOW RIGHT) TEA FOR
SORE EYES.**

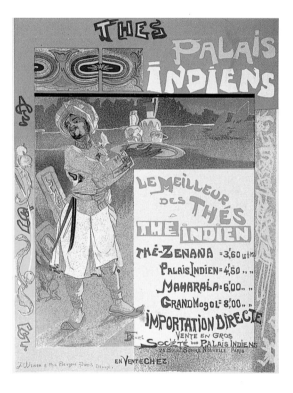

THIS IS A CARLTON BOOK

This edition published in 1999

Copyright © Carlton Books Limited 1999

ISBN hardback 1 85868 715 2
ISBN paperback 1 85868 779 9

Project Editor: Martin Corteel
Project art direction: Trevor Newman
Picture researcher: Alex Pepper
Production: Sarah Schuman
Designed by: Ros Saunders

Printed in Dubai

AUTHOR'S ACKNOWLEDGEMENTS

This is an ideal opportunity for me to thank everyone involved in the tea trade around the world who has helped me with information and advice over the past 15 years. I have been astonished again and again by the kindness and support that I have always found and am honoured to have worked in such a fascinating industry and to have made so many true friends. I cannot thank everyone by name, but this book carries my sincere gratitude and warm friendship to them all.

PICTURE CREDITS

The publishers would like to thank the following sources for their kind permission to reproduce the pictures in this book:

AKG London 12; Ancient Art & Architecture Collection 9, 10; Anthony Blake Photo Library 6; Bridgeman Art Library, London/Bonhams, London *Tea making, from an album of 23 Chinese School paintings, c.1790, Qing Dynasty (1644-1912)* 11b/British Museum, London, *View of a Dutch trading post at Dejima-Nagasaki, Nagasaki School (1720-1850)* 11t/Christopher Denniston Collection, *London Summer afternoon tea, Art-Gout-Beaute* 69tr/Johnny van Haeften Gallery, London, *The return to Amsterdam of the fleet of the Dutch East India Company in 1599 by Andries van Eertvelt (1590-1652)* 13/Private Collection, *Boston Tea Party; the 'Boston Boys' throwing the taxed tea into the Charles River, 1773 by Anonymous* 14/State Russian Museum, St Petersburg, Russia, *The Merchant's wife at tea, 1918 by Boris Mikhailovich Kustodiev 1876-1927* 15; Camera Press 5br, 92; Cephas/Alain Le Garsmeur 28, 29/Alain Proust 5tr, 82/Mick Rock 30/Stockfood 23, 26br, 27; Christie's Images 34b, 68r, 68l, 69; Corbis/Peter Johnson 53/Christine Kolisch 51/Neil Rabinowitz 96/Michael S. Yamashita 74; et Archive 2, 4tl, 8, 16, 17, 18, 19, 66; FLPA 4tr, 21, 34t; Food Features 77, 81; Robert Harding Picture Library 20, 24, 56; Hulton Getty 7; Image Bank 41b, 41t, 46, 67, 84, 90, 91; Image Select 22tl; Chris Lobina 22br, bc, bl, 70; Panos 47/Trygve Bolstad 35, 57/Jean-Leo Dugast 32, 33/Jan Hammond 47/Crispin Hughes 59/Barbara Klass 38, 39/Caroline Penn 4b, 64/Paul Quayle 37/Paul Smith 43/Sean Sprague 52; Tony Stone 3, 5tl, 36, 44, 45, 48, 54, 61, 65, 72, 76, 85, 88, 93, 95; Tea Direct 62; Twinings 5bl, 78, 87.

Every effort has been made to acknowledge correctly and contact the source and/or copyright holder of each picture, and Carlton Books Limited apologises for any unintentional errors or omissions which will be corrected in future editions of this book.

& infusions
tea

A connoisseur's guide

JANE PETTIGREW

CARLTON

CONTENTS

INTRODUCTION

Although I grew up drinking tea in England, I have to admit that I was totally ignorant about the subject until 1983 when I opened a tea shop in south-west London with two friends. Although I didn't know it then – I had pictured a daily routine of making cakes and chatting to customers – it was the beginning of the most amazing time for me.

I discovered for many different groups of people all over the world tea is not just a drink but a vital and colourful part of life. Mention tea and immediately people are drawn into discussing the blend or leaf they enjoy most, favourite porcelains and teapots, the best tea shop they've ever been to, tea parties they remember from childhood, even the plantations they've visited in exotic, far-off lands. My own research has led me down many unexpectedly exciting and fascinating paths and made me many friends all over the world.

Tea does seem to have a charisma that draws people in, brings them together in a close circle of harmony and communication. When newcomers discover its charms, lives can radically change – like mine, like that of therapists who now use tea when treating sick children and emotionally damaged patients, and like all the new tea-shop owners who gave up high-powered jobs and large salaries to serve tea to customers who then often became their friends.

For me, tea never loses its interest and I never stop learning. It has opened up an entirely new world. When colleagues and friends told me that I was making a big mistake in giving up my "proper" job in education to open a tea shop, they could not possibly have known how wrong they were!

Jane Pettigrew, *April 1999*

THE STORY OF TEA

In all my years of research, I have always read that tea is thought to have been discovered in China in 2737 BC. All the stories tell how the emperor Shennong, a herbalist and scholar, became aware of the tea plant's fragrant and refreshing properties when a few leaves drifted down from an overhanging branch into the water that the emperor was boiling in a large pan on a fire in the open air. Although there is no written proof of tea being drunk as long ago as that, the date has always figured in the accepted legend.

But recently I came across a book on tea written by a group of Chinese tea specialists and published in China which states that Shennong is regarded in Chinese folklore as a sage representing the wisdom of the Chinese people in the Zhuo period (*circa* 1100 BC). The authors mention a book on herbal medicine called *Shennong Materia Medica* which includes the following information: "Shennong came across 72 toxicated herbs daily in tasting hundreds of herbs but was antidoted by taking tea". In an encyclopaedia of Chinese history Shennong is described as "the holy father, a legendary ruler, supposed to have invented the plough and discovered the curative virtues of plants". But did Shennong really exist, and if so when? Was he a king or an emperor? Or is it not possible that the name "Shennong" was simply that of a race of Chinese people who farmed the land and knew about herbs? Perhaps the date is not of so much consequence. What is important is that the tea plant was discovered and that it originated in China where it was first taken as a herbal remedy. A legend from India claims that it was there that tea was first used to ward off sleep during meditation by the venerable Buddhist monk, Bodhidharma. The plant certainly does grow wild in India, but the Indian word "chai" actually derives from the Chinese "cha". And although there is evidence that Indians used the leaves from wild tea trees for their restorative powers, it is generally accepted that the plant was first cultivated in China.

All the tea in China

Judging by the number of ways in which the Chinese brew, drink and eat tea leaves today in different regions of their vast country, it is likely that the same variety of recipes and methods existed all those years ago. Fresh green leaves gathered from wild bushes and trees were no doubt boiled in water as an infusion, stewed with rice and herbs to make a nourishing soup, mixed as a vegetable with nuts, pickled in oil, or dried and stored for later use just as they are today. They were also used to make ointments for skin complaints, and taken as a stimulant or anti-depressant. Gradually, cultivation was introduced to satisfy a growing demand, and processing methods were developed to dry and preserve the green leaves.

By the third century BC, tea was no longer thought of simply as a herbal remedy. It was drunk by many people for pleasure throughout the day. By the third or fourth century AD, it was being presented to emperors, used as valuable currency in trade with neighbouring countries, and served at court. Manufacture by this time involved compressing steamed green leaves into cakes which were stored until needed, then baked and pounded into small pieces which were infused in porcelain pots. Onion, ginger and orange were often added as flavourings.

By the seventh and eighth centuries AD, some of the provinces that are today famous for their fine teas (Fujian, Guangdong, Hunan, Sichuan, Yunnan, Anhui) were cultivating the herb on large plantations that were often located near Buddhist temples and monasteries. The best teas (then as now) came from high mountain areas where mists fed the plants with the humidity they love and where monks devoted hours of toil to the care of the plants and the careful plucking of the leaves. After steaming, the plucked shoots were mixed with plum juice (which acted as a bonding agent) and pressed into solid, dense bricks or cakes. As in early centuries, these were then softened by roasting, crumbled, infused in boiled water and often mixed with salt, ginger, orange peel, cloves, peppermint, onions, or berries to make a hot spiced tea.

From the tenth to the twelfth centuries, dried green leaves were pulverized to a fine powder and whisked into boiled water (the form of tea-drinking that eventually made its way into Japan and became the main part of the Japanese Tea Ceremony). In the fourteenth century, loose leaf green tea became more popular and this was steeped in water just as we brew tea today. Instead of compressing the tea into cakes, the loose dried leaves were stored and transported in large earthenware containers or lacquer boxes. At first the Chinese found the leaf tea rather bitter, but brewing was much easier than it had been with the cakes or bricks and gradually, as manufacturing processes were improved towards the end of the thirteenth century, a more pleasant taste was achieved and the fashion for loose tea grew.

ABOVE

**A VIEW OF A DUTCH
TRADING POST AT
DEJIMA-NAGASAKI
(NAGASAKI SCHOOL,
1720–1850).**

RIGHT

**PACKING TEA INTO
CHESTS IN A CHINESE
FACTORY FROM AN
ALBUM OF 23 CHINESE
SCHOOL PAINTINGS**
CIRCA 1790.

The tea trade begins

By the fourteenth century AD, China was trading abroad. As long ago as 138 BC, the Chinese emperor had sent emissaries to investigate the possibilities of trade outside the country's borders. Ships sailed regularly to and from India, Ceylon and other Asian destinations. After the Arab conquests of the lands to China's west, travel along trade routes to Rome and all the countries in between spread the word about tea, as well as other sought-after commodities such as silk and spices.

Between the seventh and ninth centuries, trading was established with Korea and Japan to the east, and Persia, India, Afghanistan and Arabia to the west and south west. Tea must surely have become a staple commodity for the people of those countries in those days, and they are all major tea consumers today. We often assume that Japan was the only nation outside Britain to develop a tea-drinking ceremony, but the Arab states (Egypt and Iran are the world's third biggest consumers after Ireland and Britain) also have their own way of brewing tea with mint and serving it in little curved glasses. And Russia

(where tea was not regularly imported until the end of the seventeenth century) has its own unique way of brewing and serving tea with the elegant samovar. Perhaps the enormous distances and the hostility of the terrain had hindered trade between China and Russia during earlier centuries, and it was not until 1689 that a treaty was signed and a trading post established at the border where furs from Moscow were swapped for tea from the Chinese plantations.

It seems that the Dutch and the Portuguese were the most enterprising of the European countries. In the second half of the sixteenth century, while England was trying to build its resources after the disastrous squabbles between Catholics and Protestants, the Portuguese and the Dutch, in particular, were busy discovering coffee, tea, chocolate and tobacco, and setting up trading routes with the East. The Dutch were the first to grow the coffee plant outside Ethiopia and Yemen, and likewise with tea they were one step ahead. By the early 1600s, they were exporting Chinese tea to Holland from their trading base at Java, and regular cargoes were soon being traded to France, Germany, Belgium and Portugal. Although the British must have heard of tea or even drunk tea when abroad, there is no record of it having been available in Britain until 1658.

The Dutch traded from Java, the Portuguese had a base at the port of Macao on the southern Chinese coast, and eventually the English East India Company gained the right to set up a trading base in Canton on the Chinese mainland – but not until 1684, nearly 90 years after the Dutch had established themselves on Java. From that point on, all Britain's tea was shipped direct from China to London, while the British empire grew apace.

By the mid-1800s, most of Europe knew about tea, and some groups were drinking it as the preferred beverage. The French took to it for a short while, the Germans and the Dutch showed more interest but, whereas most decided that coffee held more appeal, Britain, Southern Ireland and much of eastern Europe had become confirmed tea drinkers.

When tea-drinking Europeans crossed the Atlantic to start a new life in the uncharted territories of North America, of course tea travelled with them. So, teapots, samovars and kettles were transported to new homes, and the brewing of a comforting cup of tea became just as commonplace in America as it had become in Europe. But when George III of England decided to impose tea import duties on his American colonies, the rebellion among his subjects there led to the Boston Tea Party, the American War of Independence and the end of American tea drinking for quite a number of years.

BELOW

**THE "BOSTON BOYS"
THROW THE MUCH-
DESPISED TAXED
TEA INTO THE CHARLES
RIVER, 1773 (BY AN
ANONYMOUS ARTIST).**

Breaking free from China

By the 1800s, much of the world was drinking tea and it almost all came from China, with a small amount exported from Japan and Indonesia. No doubt Britain would have gone on trading silver for tea with China if it had not been for two facts. China was not easy to deal with, and for some time Britain had been considering the possibility of producing her own tea elsewhere. However, the real complication was that Britain had little to offer China except cotton which the Chinese did not need or want. What they really wanted was opium, although its import was banned by the Chinese government. By this time the British owned land in India, where they produced opium commercially in the state of Bengal. By clever dealing through middlemen, the British found a way of exporting opium to China, making a great deal of money in the process. The Chinese got their opium, and no blame could be directly pinned on Britain. The money that was earned from the Chinese opium dealers was paid straight back for tea supplies. The deals continued until the Chinese government took a stand and confiscated imports, prompting Britain to declare war in 1840. Tea was no longer allowed to leave China for London's docks.

This episode could have spelled disaster for tea drinkers in Britain and elsewhere, but fortunately tea had already been found growing wild in Assam in north-eastern India. By 1823, the first plantations had been established and in 1838 the first Indian tea was shipped to Britain. Soon tea was being cultivated in other parts of north-east India, in the Kangra valley in the north west and in Travancore and Nilgiris in the south. Ceylon's plantations were developed by British planters in the 1870s but, although the export of China tea had been re-established by this time, the quantities traded with Britain were never as high as they had been before the opium wars.

The trading of tea became much quicker and easier in the 1840s after the launch of the first clippers. These sleek, stable and incredibly fast ships

knocked between five and seven months off the time it took to sail from China to Europe or North America. The clipper races that ended in the port of London after a round trip of only seven or eight months made headline news and added a premium to the first tea home. But the romance of the tea clipper era ended with the opening of the Suez Canal in 1869, and today only the *Cutty Sark* sits in stately fashion by the River Thames at Greenwich as a last reminder of the excitement of those days.

By the turn of the century, annual tea consumption in Britain alone was approximately 115,200 tons – about 6 pounds 2 ounces per person. As consumption grew, so too did the industry, and at the end of the nineteenth century the first plantings of tea had been made in Africa. By the 1940s, major plantations had been set up in Kenya, Uganda, Tanganyika (now Tanzania) and Rhodesia (now Zimbabwe). The first tea from Kenya was sold in London in 1928 and today the country ranks third in world production.

ABOVE

"THE MERCHANT'S WIFE AT TEA" (1918) BY BORIS MIKHAILOVICH KUSTODIEV (1878–1927).

OVERLEAF

SERVANTS SERVE TEA WITH BREAD AND BUTTER IN AN INDIAN HOME IN THE NINETEENTH CENTURY.

The tea bag revolution

An American by the name of Thomas Sullivan is credited with the invention of the tea bag in 1908. It apparently happened by accident when he sent out samples of his teas to customers in neat little silk bags – he was obviously a man with style. Instead of opening the bag as he had intended, and tipping the leaves into a teapot in the conventional way, the recipients steeped the entire silk bag in boiling water. They must have found the idea convenient, clean and much easier when it came to getting rid of the infused leaves, for a good number placed orders for the tea – and they wanted it in bags.

Silk gave way to gauze, the commercial production of tea bags took off in the United States in the 1920s and, by 1935, the bags were available in the familiar string and tag format (to allow the manufacturer to advertise its brand name) and in both cup and pot size. The tea bag revolution did not hit Britain until the 1960s when sales rose fast. Today tea bags account for 80 to 90 per cent of all tea consumed in Britain.

The introduction of the tea bag completely changed the face of tea in terms of production methods and drinking habits everywhere. Today, I am sad to say that many people around the world have never experienced tea brewed in any other way than in a tea bag. Sad because, by picking up the first box of tea bags that comes to hand in a supermarket, tea drinkers are automatically denying themselves the pleasure of trying some of the world's fine teas that are not packed in this way. And sad because so many tea bags are so dreadful – they do not contain enough tea, the tea is often of pretty poor quality, they are often brewed badly in haste and with impatience, and, very importantly, they deprive us of the pleasure of the ceremony of brewing and serving an excellent pot of tea. Brewing and drinking tea should be as much about the enjoyment of beautiful tea ware as about the taste and quality of the tea itself.

OPPOSITE

THE *CUTTY SARK* ON HER MAIDEN VOYAGE IN 1870 (WATERCOLOUR BY CORNELIUS DE VRIES, *CIRCA* **1973).**

FROM THE LEAF TO THE CUP

OPPOSITE
THE ISLAND OF JAVA IN INDONESIA HAS MORE THAN 33,000 ACRES OF TEA PLANTATIONS.

When you grow up in a country where black tea is drunk with milk and sometimes sugar, you assume that no other kind of tea exists. I could not believe my taste buds when I started trying the different varieties. It was like discovering wines. I became aware of green teas and oolongs and teas scented with rose petals. With time, I found that I was able to tell the difference between a Darjeeling and a high-grown Ceylon.

BELOW
THE LEAF AND FLOWER OF THE *CAMELLIA SINENSIS.*

Having discovered just a handful of the 3,000 or more types of tea that are produced all over the world (and I am still discovering new ones), for me there was no turning back. These 3,000 teas are divided into six main categories – white, green, oolong, black (the Chinese call these red teas), compressed and flavoured. Some specialists would add a seventh category – pu-erh.

All true teas (not herbal or fruit infusions or other herbal preparations) are made from the leaves or buds of the *Camellia sinensis* (also called the *Thea sinensis*). The plant is an evergreen native of China

The flowers of the tea plant are delicate and white, and when they drop a little round seed pod forms. The plant loves hot and humid conditions, preferring temperatures of between 10°C and 30°C. It will grow at just above sea level, but prefers elevations of over 1,500 metres. Height, cool mornings, hot days and misty clouds produce the finest teas.

The flavour, aroma and colour of the tea you brew also depend on a number of other factors as well as the growing conditions. They depend on when the leaves are plucked (morning, midday, spring, summer, etc.), how they are plucked (by machine or by hand), how they are processed (by hand, by machine, what sort of machine, timings, temperatures and handling), what happens to them after manufacture (are they blended, flavoured, compressed into bricks or cakes), and how carefully they are stored and packaged. A final variable is the water used for brewing, as different minerals in water can significantly alter the flavour.

and a close relative of the ornamental camellia. The tea trade generally thinks of the plant as having three subspecies – *Camellia sinensis sinensis*, *Camellia sinensis assamica* and a Cambodian species known as *Camellia assamica* subspecies *Lasiocalyx*.

Like all plants, this Chinese camellia grows differently in different climatic conditions, different soils, and under different methods of cultivation. In some areas it grows as a bush to a height of only five metres, in others, it grows as a sturdy tree, reaching heights of 15–20 metres. The size of the leaf can also vary in length from two to six centimetres. Some leaves are covered with tiny white hairs, while others are smooth and shiny. Some are long, flat and narrow, others wide and crinkly at the edges.

White tea

White teas are very rare and are seldom found outside China where they are produced in the mountain areas of Fujian Province. The little buds that form on the variety of the plant that grows there are covered in silvery hairs and these give the baby curled up leaves a white appearance. They are picked carefully by hand, either dried in the sun or gently steamed in a pan to evaporate the water content, then packed in air-tight containers. When brewed, white teas give hardly any colour at all and infuse a very delicate flavour into the water.

Green tea

The manufacturing process for green teas varies from country to country. In China, smallholder farmers still make small batches of tea by hand, while in factories the usual method of production is by machine. In both China and Japan, the new leaves are plucked either by hand or machine and carried immediately to the factory where they are withered slowly to reduce their water content. Then they are dried, steamed or pan-fried to remove more water. In between the drying or steaming, they are shaped by rolling or twisting, depending on the final appearance required. In China, leaf shapes vary from thin, crinkly eyebrow-shaped pieces, to tight balls, to flat, sharp-edged needles, to twisted pieces, to curled whole leaves. In Japan, the flat shiny blades are sometimes a rich jade green, sometimes a paler olive colour, and some are rougher in texture with almost reddish stalks and stems.

Oolong tea

Often referred to as "semi-fermented" teas, oolong teas mainly come from China and Taiwan. After the leaves have been picked and withered, they are put through a series of very careful drying, rolling and steaming and a short period of oxidation (or fermentation) that turns the leaves from green to red-brown. A very short period of 15 per cent fermentation produces what are called in China "fragrant" oolongs or pouchongs. "Amber" oolongs are 30–40 per cent fermented", while 70–80 per cent fermentation produces "white tip" oolongs. Some oolongs are shaken in bamboo baskets to lightly bruise only parts of the leaves and start the oxidation process. The finished leaf has beautiful pink edges and veins while the rest of the leaf stays green. The dry leaves of some oolongs are quite black but, as they absorb water during brewing, they develop red and deep green markings.

Black tea

Although there are many different black teas from all over the world, each with its own flavour and characteristics, all of them undergo four basic stages of manufacture – withering, rolling, oxidation and drying. The leaves are plucked by hand or by mechanical harvester and brought to a mustering point by the pickers. The pickers are paid according to the amount of leaves gathered each day so the

ABOVE

CADDY, SCOOP, BOWL AND BAMBOO WHISK USED FOR PREPARING JAPANESE GREEN TEA.

PREVIOUS PAGES
**CHINESE TEA PICKERS
LOADING THE FRESHLY
PLUCKED LEAVES ON TO
A TRUCK IN YUNNAN
PROVINCE.**

leaves are weighed before they are transported to the factory (on or near the plantation). Here the leaves are spread out in the warm air until a certain percentage of the water content has evaporated and the leaves have become soft and limp.

In some producing countries the leaves are withered in the open air, while in others factories have special withering rooms. Once the leaves have been withered, they undergo one of two processes. The orthodox method of manufacture twists and breaks the leaf but doesn't cut it up into small pieces. The surface of the leaves is broken to release the natural juices that are essential in the development of the recognizable tea flavour. In China, this

BELOW

**A BRICK OF
COMPRESSED BLACK
TEA DUST MADE
IN CHINA.**

rolling is sometimes carried out by hand, but in most factories around the world the Rotorvane machine or Lawrie Tea Processor is used. The CTC method ("cut, tear and curl") chops the leaves into very small pieces so that, when finished, the tea will brew quickly and give a strong, colour infusion. The CTC machine macerates the leaf so that it becomes a mass of small particles.

After rolling or chopping, the leaves are broken up and spread out in troughs in a cool fermenting room where they stay for three and a half to four and a half hours to react with the oxygen in the air. The chemical process that takes place turns the leaves from green to red-brown. At the end of the fermentation (or oxidation), the leaves are dried either in hot ovens or by being blown along hot air tunnels. In China, this drying process is sometimes done in a large wok, the leaves being turned by hand. At the end of the drying stage, the pieces of tea are dark brown or black and have a vaguely burnt aroma. During manufacture the polyphenols in tea undergo various changes. During fermentation, some are oxidized and give the tea its final flavour and colour. Others remain unoxidized and give the liquor its pungency and astringency.

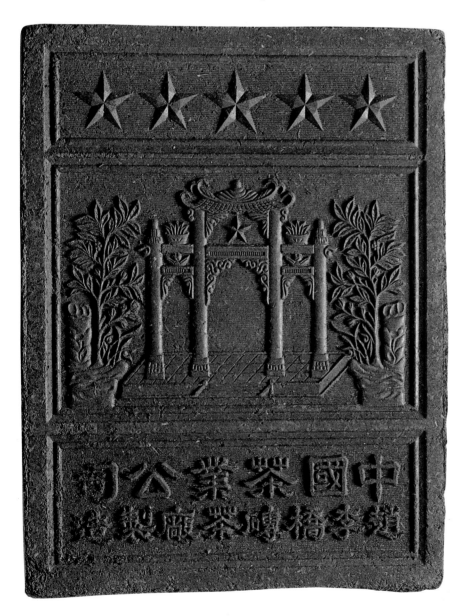

Compressed tea

Compressed tea is made by packing green, oolong or black processed tea leaves tightly together into balls, cakes or bricks. The balls are available in different sizes and are sometimes wrapped in dried grasses, sometimes in strings of five. The cakes are made in several forms – tiny little nests each wrapped carefully in paper, larger bird's nest shapes individually packaged in cloth or paper, or large or small flat round slabs. Flat rectangular bricks (similar to those used in the trade centuries ago) are hydraulically made using very fine tea dust. On one side is usually a typical Chinese design of a temple or gateway, and on the other markings that divide the slab into small portions rather like a bar of chocolate.

Flavoured tea

Ever since the first teas were enjoyed for pleasure in China, a variety of flavourings have been added, such as peach leaves, onions, spices, orange peel and berries. Tea easily absorbs other tastes and aromas, offering endless possibilities for different flavours. Today, the Chinese produce flavoured teas using green, pouchong or black teas scented with orchids, jasmine flowers, rose petals, honeysuckle, bergamot, magnolia, gardenia and osmanthus.

In the Arab world, green and black teas are often flavoured with mint, while the Indians make chai by boiling black tea leaves with cardamoms and other spices, sugar and milk. The idea of flavoured teas is highly fashionable in North America and Europe, where an extensive range is available – from apricot, banana, or caramel through to raisin, sticky toffee pudding and vanilla. The teas are blended after the normal manufacturing process is finished. The additional flavourings are added either in the form of granules which release their flavour slowly into the tea, or as a liquid that is sprayed on to the leaves while they are tumbled in a large drum.

Pu-erh tea

Pu-erh (or Puer) tea can be loose leaf or compressed. It is made from the leaves of what the Chinese call pu-erh cha, their name for the subspecies *Camellia sinensis assamica*. Geographically, Assam and Pu-erh are not particularly far away from each other, and this fact plus the use in both places of the same subspecies explains why tea from Pu-erh has a similar strength and pepperiness to Assam tea. But, the tea producers in Pu-erh add an earthy flavour to their tea by fermenting it twice and then storing it to give it time to mature. The brew produced is dark and strong and said to be very healthy and good for the digestion.

ABOVE
**GRADING THE TEA IN
HANGZHOU, CHINA.**

Sorting and grading

The last stages of all tea manufacture are sorting – the removal of unwanted pieces of stalk or woody stem – and grading. This is carried out either by hand or machine. All teas must be graded into different-sized pieces of leaf. This is because different sizes of tea particle infuse at different rates (the general rule is the smaller the piece, the quicker it brews, and vice versa). If a mixture of sizes is used to make a pot of tea, the infusion will not give a uniform strength and flavour. When a blend of teas is created using teas from various sources to give a chosen character, all the pieces of tea must be the same size, otherwise the balance of flavour will be lost in the packet when the smaller pieces sink to the bottom.

Finished tea is sorted into "leaf" and "broken leaf" grades – known as "pekoe" and "broken pekoe" – with all sorts of sub-divisions to denote size, appearance and colour. The word "pekoe" comes from the Chinese Amoy dialect word that describes the fine silvery hairs on the underside of the leaf or the soft tips of young buds. These are a few of the different categories by which black teas are normally graded (see page 31):

OVERLEAF
**TUOCHA – COMPRESSED
BLACK TEA MADE IN
CHINA IN THE FORM OF
A SMALL BIRD'S NEST.**

RIGHT
**DIFFERENT GRADES OF
BLACK TEA RANGING
FROM THE BEST,
BROKEN ORANGE PEKOE,
TO THE SMALLEST
GRADE, FANNINGS.**

❖ **Flowery Orange Pekoe (FOP)**
High-quality tea made from the end bud and one new leaf.

❖ **Golden Flowery Orange Pekoe (GFOP)**
The same as Flowery Orange Pekoe but with lots of little golden tips (these are the lighter-coloured ends of the buds and leaves that do not darken during manufacture).

❖ **Tippy Golden Flowery Orange Pekoe (TGFOP)**
Flowery Orange Pekoe with a higher proportion of tips.

❖ **Finest Tippy Golden Flowery Orange Pekoe (FTGFOP)**
Exceptionally high-quality tea with plenty of little golden tips.

❖ **Orange Pekoe (OP)**
Long, pointed leaves plucked as the buds open into leaf.

❖ **Pekoe (P)**
Shorter pieces of leaf than Orange Pekoe.

❖ **Pekoe Souchong (PS)**
Short, coarse pieces of leaf.

Note: Pekoe Souchong and Souchong are the coarsest grades.

The broken grades fall into the same categories as the leaf grades (Golden Flowery Broken Orange Pekoe, Broken Orange Pekoe, and so on.) with the addition of "Fannings" and "Dusts". These are the finest pieces of leaf that are left after the leaf and broken grades have been sorted. CTC manufacture has led to the introduction of further sub-divisions. These very small pieces of leaf give a quick coloury brew and are generally used in tea bags.

Green teas are graded by which part of the plant was plucked to make the tea – one bud, one bud wrapped by a leaf, one open leaf and a bud, one bud and two leaves, and so on. Good quality green teas have leaf and bud in one piece. Generally lower grades contain broken pieces of leaf and bits of stem rather than whole leaves.

The role of the tea taster

Every tea factory, every broking house and every blending and packing company employs a team of tea tasters. In the factory, the tasters are responsible for checking the quality of the teas and for describing them ready for sale. In the broking houses, the tasters assess samples of teas sent in from producers around the world in order to decide their value and suitability for various potential buyers. In the blending and packing companies, the tasters have to decide which teas to buy from producers or brokers so that they can order the teas they need to supply their customers with single-estate teas and blends.

To taste the tea, tasters carefully measure out exact amounts of loose leaf tea into white porcelain brewing cups, and pour on an exact amount of boiling water, then allow the tea to infuse for a precise period of time – usually six minutes. They then tip the infusion into a tasting bowl, and tip the infused leaf on to the lid of the brewing cup. Sometimes they add an exact measure of milk to the liquor. The taster then sucks a spoonful of tea sharply into the mouth, swills it around and then spits it out into a mobile spittoon that is trundled up and down beside the tasting bench as he works.

The taster's assessment is based on the appearance of the dry leaf, the appearance and smell of the infused leaf, the colour and appearance of the liquor, and the taste. There is an entire vocabulary of words used to describe taste, appearance and all the other characteristics that are assessed. Simply by tasting, an experienced taster can tell you just about all there is to know about the tea, including the height at which it was grown, the time of day it was picked, the weather on that day, even (as some tasters joke) the state of the tea factory manager's marriage (poor-quality tea, they presume, is produced by a manager whose mind was elsewhere). Amusingly, despite the fact that the tasters spend their entire day tasting and spitting and lining their mouths with tannin, when it's time for a break, they stop – for a cup of tea!

OVERLEAF

A TEA TASTER IN A SRI LANKAN FACTORY CAREFULLY EXAMINES THE DRY LEAF AS WELL AS THE LIQUOR AND THE INFUSED TEA.

RIGHT
**COMPRESSED TEA
IN AN ORNATE
PRESENTATION CASE.**

BELOW
**ENGLISH TEA CADDIES
FROM THE LATE
EIGHTEENTH CENTURY
MADE IN
TORTOISESHELL (*LEFT*),
·PEARWOOD (*CENTRE*)
AND SATINWOOD.
BECAUSE TEA WAS
EXPENSIVE, ALL SUCH
CADDIES HAD A LOCK.**

Storing and packaging

In the past, as soon as finished tea came out of the dryers at the end of the manufacturing process, and had been graded, it was packed into tea chests. These wooden boxes are now only used for large-leaf quality teas, while small-leaf teas are now stored and transported in strong paper sacks. When filled, these are stacked on pallets, wrapped with plastic and loaded into containers ready for transportation by sea to customers all over the world.

Some tea companies buy direct from the factory, whereas others purchase through brokers who operate for them at the world tea auctions. As well as selling in bulk via these channels, some factories also pack their own tea into packets, caddies or gift boxes ready for sale direct to customers at home and abroad.

Some tea plantations and gardens in certain countries produce excellent quality teas which connoisseurs seek out for their very special characteristics. These teas are not always available or may be available only in small quantities. They may also be expensive and, like wines, do not taste exactly the same each year – because of variations in weather patterns and conditions. These teas are sold as single-estate teas with their name proudly displayed on the packaging. They may be sold direct from the estate to private customers or through brokers and retailers.

Other teas are not good as "self-drinkers". They need to be blended with other teas to create a palatable drink with strength and flavour. These types of teas are known as fillers and go into house specialities such as breakfast and afternoon blends.

To create a house blend, tasters select from up to 35 different teas to give consistent flavour, body, strength and colour. Each time they make up the recipe for that particular blend, the balance of different teas may change – again depending on the characteristics of the teas available.

For home blending, there are no rules. You can simply mix different teas together until you find a taste and strength that you like. Add flavourings that

suit you – for example a stick of cinnamon or a vanilla pod in a caddy of tea adds a pleasant flavour and aroma. I recently discovered a green Sencha tea from Japan flavoured with vanilla and you won't get me to drink anything else after dinner these days. It is wonderful – light, slightly sweet and so refreshing.

Putting the tea in the tea bag

There are a number of important factors involved in making good tea bags. The paper or fibre used for the bag must not add any flavour to the infused tea. The size of the perforations must allow the water to seep in and the tea solubles to seep out into the boiling water, and the amount of tea must be correct to give as good a cup of tea as could be brewed from loose leaves and the bag must be big enough to allow the leaves to swell during infusion and give off their flavour.

Traditional tea bag papers are made from Manila hemp which is manufactured specially for use in high-speed packing machines (today's machines can produce up to 1,200 bags per minute). Tea bags come square, round, rectangular, pyramidal, gusseted or flat, heat sealed or stapled, tagged or plain. The shape and all the other visual details are really totally irrelevant – what matters far more is the quality and quantity of the tea inside, and the care with which it is stored and brewed.

TEA AROUND THE WORLD

Until the early part of the nineteenth century, China, Japan and Indonesia were the only countries producing tea on a commercial scale. Since the 1830s, there has been a steady expansion of the industry in many developing countries, particularly in India, Sri Lanka and parts of Africa where tea has become a major product that supplies both domestic and export markets. Total world production is over 2,600,000 tonnes of tea every year.

Australia

The Australian tea industry is very small, producing around 1,500 tons a year. All the estates produce black tea and one (Madura Tea Estates) also produces some green. The first tea bushes were planted at Melbourne's Botanical Gardens in 1824, but commercial production did not really get going until the early 1960s when plantations were established on Mount Bartle Frere, Australia's highest mountain. Today tea is also being grown in New South Wales, in Victoria and on the island of Tasmania. The black teas are mainly CTC.

Argentina

Most of Argentina's tea is grown in the provinces of Misiones and Corrientes in the north east of the country. Tea cultivation started in 1951 as a development of the production of yerba maté, a herbal infusion made from the leaves of the *Ilex Paraguayensis* tree. Labour shortages have led to the development of mechanical harvesters, and growers are making every effort to manufacture teas that are competitive in terms of quality and price. Argentine teas give a strong, black infusion with an earthy flavour. They are most commonly used in blending or in the production of instant tea.

Azores

The Portuguese introduced tea as an ornamental plant to the Azores island of San Miguel in the 1820s. Some 50 years later, seeds from the plants were used to establish plantations and production grew. By the first half of the twentieth century there were 300 hectares under tea and 14 small processing factories. However, because of a shortage of labour and a lack of real understanding of tea cultivation and production, all but five of the factories were closed by the 1960s and plantations were neglected. In 1984, a rehabilitation programme began. Plants from India were introduced and orthodox black teas are once again being manufactured.

Bangladesh

Tea cultivation in Bangladesh (once part of India) started in the 1840s, shortly after the British set up the first Assam plantations. The main growing areas lie to the east of the Ganga-Jumma flood plain close to India's Cachar tea district, and most of the gardens are only just above sea level, which is unusual for tea. About 80 per cent of the crop is manufactured between June and November and, whereas in the past traditional orthodox manufacture was used,

there has been a switch since the late 1960s to almost 99 per cent CTC black tea production. Bangladesh teas are similar in quality to other plain-grown teas from Cachar and Dooars in India.

Brazil

Tea was introduced to Brazil by Dom João VI in 1812 when 6,000 bushes were planted in the Botanical Garden of Rio de Janeiro. Commercial plantations followed in São Paulo, Caeté and Ouro Preto in the state of Minas Gerais. Production reached its peak in 1852, but declined rapidly after the abolition of slavery. Then, in the 1920s, a Japanese immigrant, Torazo Okamoto, smuggled some Assam tea seeds into Brazil from Ceylon and these were planted in the Vale do Ribiera on the southern coast of São Paulo. By 1984, annual output had reached 9,308 metric tons, 90 per cent of which was exported to Britain and the United States. Today, production is in decline, but the country still produces black CTC teas which are considered useful as fillers in blends.

Cameroon

The Republic of Cameroon, developed from the German West African Colony of Kamerun, lies on the central west African coast and grows tea on the fertile slopes of Mount Cameroon in the south west of the country. Commercial production started in 1914, but was overshadowed by the importance of rubber, bananas and oil palm. In the 1950s, tea gradually emerged as an important cash crop and, by 1968, Tole (on the south eastern slope of the mountain) became the main growing area, producing around 622 tons of black tea a year. There are now plantations at Ndu in North West Province and Djuttitsa in the French-speaking West Province. Most teas are black CTCs which are sold to neighbouring Tschad and Sudan and to France, Britain and other parts of Europe.

China

It has always been difficult to learn all the details of Chinese tea production. The country is vast, the languages are diverse and the Chinese have traditionally guarded their secrets very closely. However, we do know that 18 provinces across the southern half of the country produce tea. Many smallholder farmers still grow and manufacture small amounts of green tea for local consumption, processing the leaves by hand. Larger plantations produce leaf that is manufactured in factories and sold through provincial corporations. The Chinese themselves drink green teas (and sometimes oolongs) and all black teas are produced only for export. The manufacture of black leaf developed in the seventeenth century in the days when China's export markets around the world were growing. Producers and merchants discovered that by drying, fermenting and firing the leaf, it kept and travelled better, thus guarding against loss of earnings due to spoilt stock.

China produces white, green, oolong, black, pu-erh, compressed and flavoured teas. Because the country is so vast and in some parts impenetrable, it is really impossible to know how many different teas are produced. However, tea-making is taken very seriously and there are very clear guidelines in manuals for picking, withering, rolling, hand-shaping and drying the tea. For example, to make Lung Ching tea – one of China's top quality green teas – no less than 25 processes and 10 different hand movements are involved.

The names of Chinese teas can be confusing because of the different languages and dialects that are used, and their different English spellings. Names can be based on the history of the particular tea, the area where it is produced, a legend that explains its origins, the method of manufacture, the time of year when the leaves are gathered, or the grade of the leaf.

Although connoisseurs around the world seek out the best that China can offer, tea is not always the most financially rewarding crop. Farmers are beginning to turn to more lucrative options – a sad fact if we reflect on the long history of tea in China.

RIGHT

A TEAHOUSE IN WUZHEN, ZHEJIANG PROVINCE, CHINA.

BELOW

A PLANTATION AT ZANGZHON, CHINA. UNUSUALLY THE PLANTERS ARE MEN.

Ecuador

Most of Ecuador's tea is grown at Te Sangay, the first plantation to be laid out in the country in 1962. The estate lies 1,000 metres above sea level near the Andes on the edge of the Amazon Jungle, and 200 miles south east of the capital, Quito. The equatorial climatic conditions give the tea plants the heat and humidity that they love. Since 1984, a British investment programme has enabled the rehabilitation of plants and the installation of new machinery in the factory to produce CTC tea and to pack tea bags. Approximately 1,000 tons of tea are sold each year to the United States and Latin America.

India

After China, India produces more tea than any other country. There are three main growing areas, Assam and Darjeeling in the north east, and the Nilgiris in the south. There are smaller areas of production in the Kangra Valley (to the north of Delhi), Dooars (south of Assam and Darjeeling), Sikkim (north of Darjeeling) and Terai and Travancore in the south. The traditional orthodox process has gradually given way to CTC production, but the best gardens still make beautiful, much sought-after orthodox teas.

Darjeeling is a small town that lies 6,000 feet above sea level in the foothills of the Himalayan mountains. In the area around, 86 tea gardens produce some of the most exquisite teas in the world. The tea owes its unique character to the cool moist climate, the altitude at which the bushes grow, the rainfall, the well-drained sloping terrain and the minerals in the soil. The brewed tea is a light golden infusion with a delicate aroma and the subtle flavour of green muscatel grapes.

The plants only produce new shoots in the warm and humid months of the spring, summer and early autumn. The first flush of April has an astringency and flowery taste that is similar to green teas. The second flush that is gathered from May

onwards has a rounder, more mellow flavour and gives more colour in the cup. Monsoon teas, picked from mid-July to September, are stronger and are used in breakfast and other blends. Autumnal teas are produced in October and November and produce a light copper-coloured liquor and a delicate flavour. The leaves are processed in the orthodox way and are sold either by direct sale or through brokers.

Although tea was found growing wild in Assam in the 1820s, nobody believed that the native plant could be used for commercial production, so seedlings from China were brought in and planted instead. But they did not thrive and eventually the Assam subspecies was cultivated with great success, so that by the late 1830s, Indian tea was being shipped home to Britain.

Here in the land of the one-horned rhino, tea plantations stretch along both sides of the Brahmaputra valley in a climate that is hot, wet and sticky. Assam produces both orthodox and CTC teas that give a wonderful rich rounded flavour and a deep red liquor that is excellent at breakfast time.

Nilgiri tea is grown in the Blue Mountains that run down the south-western tip of India. The gardens lie at altitudes of 1,000–2,500 metres in spectacular countryside. The teas are manufactured by both the orthodox and CTC methods, and the high elevations give the liquors a fine brisk flavour with good body and a fragrant aroma.

Indonesia

By the early eighteenth century, tea plantations had been set up by the Dutch in Java. The crop was then planted in Sumatra and, in recent years, production has also started in Sulawesi. In 1992, Indonesia produced 160,000 tons of tea and exported 120,000 – 12 per cent of the total world export volume. The islands manufacture green, black and jasmine scented teas, which are very popular in the domestic market. Traditionally, orthodox manufacture was used for black teas, but 10 CTC factories now operate and produce more than 15,000 tons of CTC tea

OPPOSITE

DARJEELING TEAS ARE GROWN AT HEIGHTS OF UP TO 6,000 FEET IN THE FOOTHILLS OF THE HIMALAYAS.

**TEA GROWS IN
SWEEPING WAVES
ACROSS THE JAPANESE
COUNTRYSIDE BENEATH
MOUNT FUJI.**

LEFT

**GATHERING THE LEAVES
IN JAVA, INDONESIA.**

a year. These black teas are exported to Britain, the United States, the Netherlands, Russia, Poland, Australia, the Middle East, Pakistan and Japan. Ready-to-drink jasmine tea is packed in cartons and bottles and marketed to Indonesian consumers.

be made into ordinary Sencha or Bancha teas is processed through a series of machines which sort, cut, steam, shape, roll and polish the needles so that they emerge as short, flat, shiny olive green needles.

Making the best quality tea, Gyokuro, takes much more time and trouble. The bushes are shaded for 21 days prior to plucking, to slow the development of the leaf and concentrate the chlorophyll content, thus producing a much sweeter, more intense flavour. After plucking, the leaves are steamed, dried and rolled until they become flat dark green needles. Matcha, the powdered green tea that is served during the tea ceremony, is made by grinding Gyokuro leaf in traditional stone mills or in electrically operated grinders. Genmaicha is Bancha that has been mixed with popped corn and toasted rice, and Houjicha is Sencha or Bancha that has been roasted to give a sweet-tasting brown leaf.

Japan

Tea made its way to Japan when Buddhist monks returned from China after studying there, bringing with them the plant and news about how effective the drink was in warding off sleepiness during meditation. For this reason, as in China, the earliest plantations were often established around Buddhist temples and monasteries, and the plants were lovingly tended by the monks. Commercial cultivation on a wider scale started in the twelfth century and the plucked leaf was steamed and compressed by the Chinese method at a time when the Chinese were actually changing to a system of roasting loose leaf tea. The Japanese Tea Ceremony (*Chanoyu*) was developed in the fourteenth and fifteenth centuries and continued the fashionable Chinese tradition of serving whipped, powdered green tea, although in China this had been replaced by the infusing of loose leaf tea.

Cultivation increased rapidly in the 1950s and 60s and today the main plantations are in the southeastern corner north of Kyushu, and in the central part of the island. The Japanese produce only green tea and, after picking by machine, the leaf that is to

Kenya

As in other African countries, tea dates back to the early years of the twentieth century when production was carried out on a small scale. During the 1950s, the government realized the potential of the

BELOW

**KENYA'S TEA BUSHES
PUSH OUT NEW
SHOOTS THROUGHOUT
THE YEAR.**

crop and established the Tea Board of Kenya in order to develop and promote the industry. In 1992, Kenya held third place in world production and in exports.

The plantations are in the Kenya Highlands high up above Lake Victoria which plays an important part in creating favourable weather patterns for the tea. Warm wet air rises from the lake and travels north east toward Kericho. There it meets a prevailing wind and this provokes rainfall over the mountains – a welcome fact since much of Kenya is far too dry for the cultivation of tea.

Most of the growers are smallholder farmers who sell their leaf to local factories for manufacture. Because of the temperate climate, the bushes can

be plucked throughout the year and the factories produce excellent quality black CTC teas, most of which are exported to Britain. The tiny black grains of tea give a rich red, full-flavoured liquor with body and strength.

Malawi

Malawi's first plantations were laid out at the start of the twentieth century. The main growing areas are in the southern region of Mulanje at a height of only 500 metres above sea level. Growth of the plants is limited during the long, cold winter

months and 80 per cent of the crop is harvested in the first five months of the year when rainfall is heavy and temperatures reach 37°C. Because of the long period of dormancy and the rapid sprouting in the warmer months, Malawi's teas are very different from the teas of India or Sri Lanka. The industry has been adding carefully bred clonal plants to their existing stock and these are giving better yields and higher quality teas than before. CTC manufacture produces small leaf teas that give clear, bright, coppery-coloured liquors with good body and full flavour. Most are used as fillers in blends.

Malaysia

In 1929, John Russell persuaded the Malayan government to grant him use of a piece of land 1,750 metres up in the Cameron Highlands and then started work to create Malaya's first tea plantation. He named the estate Boh after Bohea in China which exported a great deal of tea to Britain in the seventeenth and eighteenth centuries. Today, Russell's grand-daughter, Caroline Russell, manages an estate which, with 1,200 hectares, is four times bigger than the original area. She oversees the production of 4 million kilograms of tea every year and the cultivation of oil palm, cocoa, citrus fruits and coffee. The teas are black orthodox and give a clear, coloury infusion with a smooth, light flavour, not unlike a fair quality Ceylon. They drink well without milk.

Nepal

It is thought that Nepal started to grow tea round about the same time that estates were being developed in Darjeeling in north-east India. Some bushes appear to date back to the middle of the nineteenth century, although most were planted in the 1970s. Two types of tea are produced in Nepal – high-grown tea from the eastern hills just across the border from Darjeeling, and black CTC teas from Terai which spans the Indian border. Most of the high growns are of good quality and are sold at good prices to Germany. The plantations have recently been privatized and it is hoped that this will lead to rejuvenation of the estates and improved quality.

Papua New Guinea

An experimental tea station was established in Papua New Guinea in the 1930s, but no commercial production took place until 20 years later when the Department of Agriculture built a small tea factory at Garina in Morobe Province. The real development of the industry took place in the 1960s when plantations of notable size were set up in various locations, mostly with seed from the original Garina research station. Picking is done by mechanical harvesters since there has always been a shortage of labour. Six factories operate today, producing black CTC teas for sale to Australia, South Africa, the United States, Britain, Malaysia and Sri Lanka.

Peru

Tea seeds were first planted in Peru in 1913, but the experiment was abandoned two years later. The next attempt to establish a Peruvian tea industry was in 1928 when the government brought in tea experts from Ceylon to advise and oversee cultivation. This led to an expansion of the area under tea and the setting up of new plantations in other areas. By 1942, two factories had been built, the industry developed and today 2,500 hectares of land produce around 1,600 tons of black tea a year. The main areas are in the Departments of Cusco and Huanuco where the factories run by large co-operatives have the capacity to process up to several hundred tons of tea a day. In other areas, small companies handle just two or three tons of green leaf a day. The black orthodox teas are sold as loose leaf or tea bags and are mostly consumed inside Peru.

Russia

The first attempts to grow tea in Russia date back to the middle of the nineteenth century when plantations in Georgia and Krasnodar regions were established. The tea that was produced was not very good and was blended with better-quality imported teas. In the past, processing factories were located some distance from the plantations and the necessary transportation and storage of fresh leaf in damp conditions led to the manufacture of poor teas.

Since the break-up of the Russian Empire, processing equipment and packing facilities have been improved. The newly formed Tea Association of Russia (founded in 1996) is playing an essential part in developing and stabilizing the industry.

Rwanda

During the 1990s, Rwanda suffered greatly from political unrest and civil war. Tea factories were abandoned or wrecked, and crops were destroyed or neglected. Since 1995, foreign investment has helped to rebuild the industry, and now most of the factories have been rehabilitated. New fermenting units and dryers have been installed and crops have been nurtured back to health. The main problem has been the silting up of drainage systems on the swampy land, due to neglect, but it is anticipated that both quality and quantity will soon return to normal levels.

South Africa

Commercial cultivation of tea started in 1877 in Natal, and at the beginning of the twentieth century KwaZulu-Natal established further plantations. Expansion was slow until the 1960s when new areas were planted in the Eastern Transvaal and Transkei. About 12,000 tons of black CTC teas are produced every year from leaf that is gathered between November and March and the most famous, Zulu tea (from Ntingwe Tea Estate 1,000 metres up in the hills of KwaZulu-Natal), is available in Britain and elsewhere as a single-source tea. It has a grainy appearance and gives a flavoursome and robust brew.

South Africa also produces Rooibosch, a herbal infusion made from the leaves of *Aspalathus Linoaris* which is caffeine free, rich in proteins, minerals and vitamin C. The infusion looks rather like tea and has a similar taste.

PREVIOUS PAGES
**SRI LANKA'S FINEST
TEAS ARE PRODUCED
FROM BUSHES THAT
GROW ABOVE 4,000 FEET
IN THE SOUTHERN
CENTRAL PART OF
THE ISLAND.**

RIGHT
**TAIWAN HAS BEEN A
MAJOR PRODUCER OF
OOLONGS AND
LAPSANG SOUCHONG
TEA FOR OVER
140 YEARS.**

Sri Lanka

The tear-drop shaped island of Ceylon, as Sri Lanka was once called, grows teas in six areas at altitudes ranging from 70 metres to 2,500 metres. The best teas come from Uva, Nuwara Eliya and Dimbula which all lie at higher elevations.

The distinct character of Uva teas – a wonderfully fragrant aroma and a smooth intense taste – is the result of the hot dry Cachan winds that sweep in from the north east and concentrate the flavour in the leaves.

Nuwara Eliya lies at the foot of Sri Lanka's highest mountain and is surrounded by steep mountain ridges. Although the infusions from the teas that grow there do not have much depth of colour, they have a distinct perfume and burst with flavour.

The famous Dimbulas are produced in the largest tea-growing district in the south-western corner of the central mountains. Dimbula's teas are light and aromatic with the special flavour that develops at such high elevations.

The lower regions of Ratnapura and Matara in the south west produce reasonable teas that can be useful to add quality to much poorer teas. Kandy, the ancient cultural capital, was once the centre of the planting country – first for coffee and then for tea. Plantations around the town grow teas that are rather similar to Assam teas and give a rich colour and a hint of maltiness

There has been much discussion among Sri Lankan growers over the past few years as to whether the island should increase its CTC manufacture to meet modern demands from tea-bag using countries. For now, many producers are continuing to produce their wonderful orthodox black teas that have character, quality, flavour and aroma and give clear, golden infusions.

Taiwan

Tea production started in Formosa (as it was then called) in the 1850s when tea growers from the Chinese Province of Fujian emigrated to the island.

They took with them some tea shoots and their knowledge and continued manufacturing teas in their native traditional manner. The climate was perfect, the soil rich and well-drained, and the plants thrived. Fujian is well known for its oolongs and Lapsang Souchongs, the teas for which Taiwan is now also famous. The plantations lie in the plains of the northern and western central part of the island, but the best oolongs are made with leaves that grow high up on the fertile slopes of Mount Dung Ding in the centre of Taiwan.

Tanzania

Tea was first grown by German settlers in Tanzania in 1905, but there was no commercial cultivation until 1926. The first factory was built in the Southern Highlands in 1930. Now, most of the tea is grown by smallholders in the central southern and central northern parts of the country. The leaf is collected once or twice a day from the smallholdings and transported by truck or trailer to the factories. There are 21 factories which produce CTC black teas that are sold through world auctions and by direct sale. The teas vary according to region and the best give a strong and fruity infusion.

BELOW

THE HARVESTED LEAF IS WEIGHED AT MUFINGA TEA PLANTATION IN TANZANIA.

Uganda

Uganda started growing tea in 1900, but little commercial development took place until the 1920s. The industry then expanded rapidly in the 1950s, on land owned mainly by British planters. The first licence was granted to an African planter in 1952. By the early 1970s, tea was Uganda's fourth most important export, but the political problems of the 1970s and 80s led to an almost total demise of the tea industry. With the return of peace in 1986, plantations were rehabilitated and the total amount of tea produced rose from 544,000 kilograms in 1983 to 3,948,000 kilograms in 1993. Most of the black CTC teas are marketed through the Mombasa auctions, but prices tend to be low because quality is inconsistent. The industry still suffers from a shortage of labour, irregular power supplies, lack of modern equipment in factories and a lack of funds for research.

USA

Charleston Tea Plantation, the only tea plantation in the United States, has been growing tea since 1987. A few attempts to grow the crop were made in the nineteenth century, but none of them led to commercial production. Tea is now being grown successfully on Wadmalaw Island where the sandy, well-drained soils and the hot, humid summers provide ideal growing conditions. The leaves are gathered every 15–18 days, from May to the end of October, and are then processed in the normal way. The area under tea is being developed and the growers hope to be able to increase yields.

Vietnam

For hundreds of years, tea has been growing in Vietnam. Until the end of the nineteenth century, only green tea was manufactured by hand by small-holder farmers for local consumption. Mechanized factory production developed in the early part of the twentieth century, and in the 1950s black tea manufacture was introduced. However, two thirds of all tea made is still green. Most of the plantations are in the north of the country and the growing season lasts from the end of March to December.

The Vietnamese War led to the destruction and neglect of both plants and factories, and the industry struggled on, surprisingly producing some very good quality teas, until the early 1990s. Recent investment programmes and joint ventures with the West have enabled the upgrading of factories and the improvement of tea quality. The black teas give a pleasant neutral infusion and are ideal for blending or as a base for flavoured teas. The bulk of the teas are exported to Germany, Poland and Eastern bloc countries.

Zimbabwe

Rhodesia (as Zimbabwe was previously called) was one of several African countries to start growing tea in the late 1800s. Today, there is a shortage of labour for the country's tea and coffee plantations and research programmes run by the Tea Research Foundation for Central Africa are trying to improve mechanical harvesting. The hand shears that were initially used gave green leaf that was of variable quality, and instead, small machines have been imported from Japan which are now producing much better quality leaf. However, rising labour costs and shortages of skilled labour make it difficult for the country to remain competitive.

Other tea-producing areas

Small amounts of tea are also grown in Bolivia, Burundi, CIS, Ethiopia, Guatemala, Iran, Madagascar, Mauritius, Mozambique, Tibet, Turkey and Zaire. Teas produced in these areas are usually consumed locally or are used as fillers in blends.

Speciality blends

Most tea-blending and packing companies create blends that are special to them and are devised for the preferences of their particular customers. In Russia, for example, the blends are made up of strong black teas; in Ireland, the largest tea consuming country in the world, traditional blends give a robust flavour and a strong dark liquor that is drunk with milk; the Arabs drink a lighter blend flavoured with mint. Companies in each country adapt the balance of blends to suit these variations in local preference.

The names given to speciality blends say much for the creativity of individual companies, but one thing British blenders are not allowed to do is use the names of living members of the royal family. You may still find Queen Anne tea or Duke of Wellington blend on the shelves of some stores, but Prince of Wales or Queen Mother's Favourite Blend would be strictly forbidden.

Breakfast blends

There was a time when Keemun, a black tea from China, was considered the perfect English breakfast tea. It does go well with lighter breakfast dishes, such as scrambled eggs or muffins or croissants, but most breakfast blends now usually contain teas from Assam for colour and strength, Ceylon for character and sparkle, and Africa for depth and robustness. This sort of mixture is quite potent and goes well with strong flavoured foods, such as fried bacon and egg, smoked fish or strong citrus marmalades.

Irish breakfast blends tend to include more of the Assam and African CTC teas and are therefore dark, very strong, deep coppery-red in colour and generously rich in flavour. But there are no hard and fast rules as to which tea should be the first of the day. As diets and tastes have changed over the years, so individual choices of preferred breakfast teas have begun to vary.

Afternoon blends

If you want a refreshing cup of tea in the middle of the afternoon, almost any of the lighter tea blends satisfy, so blenders often mix lightly astringent Darjeelings with high-grown, golden-flavoured Ceylons or China blacks such as Keemun. Sometimes bergamot or jasmine is added to give a gentle, refreshing perfume.

If an afternoon blend is to be taken with sandwiches, scones and pastries, a slightly richer blend will marry better. This kind of blend usually includes a mixture of Ceylon, China Yunnan (a slightly peppery black tea from Yunnan Province), Assam or quality Indonesian teas.

It is only by tasting different blends and pairing them with favourite afternoon tea foods that personal preferences can develop. Choices may also be affected by the time of the year, the weather or the mood of the occasion. Most companies offer four o'clock/five o'clock or afternoon blends, so try different varieties. Or try mixing different leaves to create an individual blend.

Earl Grey is probably the most popular blend in the world. It was originally a Chinese recipe of black teas mixed with bergamot oil, but today most blends also contain teas from elsewhere. More and more Earl Grey oolongs and Earl Grey greens are appearing on the market. The bergamot is a citrus Chinese fruit rather like a small pear-shaped orange, which is today grown commercially in Italy. The essential oil is sprayed on to the blended leaves in a large drum to ensure that all the leaves absorb their fair share of flavouring. It is really important to get the balance of bergamot right. Some blends are almost soapy because they contain too much, others taste as if they have barely come into contact with any bergamot at all.

The trend for flavoured teas is growing around Europe and North America, and an ever-increasing range is now available from even the most traditional, top-quality tea merchants. Flavourists continue to come up with extraordinary ideas; one of the latest flavours for the end of the twentieth century is apparently going to be pitahaja – a rare exotic fruit that Europe has not tasted before.

LEFT
IN MOROCCO, THE TEA
LEAVES ARE INFUSED
WITH FRESH MINT, THEN
POURED FROM A HEIGHT
INTO SMALL GLASSES.

Organic teas

As with other crops, producers who are increasingly concerned for the environment and for a better ecological balance are turning to organic methods of agriculture. This means more than simply doing away with the use of chemical fertilizers, pesticides and herbicides. It means seeking out ways to harness natural forces to control such problems as pests and weeds, using methods that do not put human health at risk, using renewable resources, protecting wildlife and maintaining the fertility of the soil.

Organically grown foods come under the strictest possible controls from international certification organizations. It takes three years of inspections, tests and visits before any tea plantation can advertise itself as certified organic. Several estates in India are now producing excellent organic teas. Look out for Ambootia, Seeyok and Makaibari organic teas from Darjeeling, and Banaspaty organic from Assam.

Fair Trade tea

It has always been of concern to many people around the world that it is seldom the workers who receive the profits for their hard work, but the owners and middle men. Fair Trade is aiming to change all that. By drawing up agreements between Fair Trade organizations in the consuming countries and the growers and producers in the countries of origin, some of the profits now go to improving the lives of the tea pickers and factory workers on some estates. The money is being used to improve housing, set up pension schemes, organize training programmes, buy ambulances and other medical facilities, run crèches and generally support the welfare of the people and the area. The use of money is strictly regulated and carefully monitored. A joint body, made up of representatives from the labour force and management, decides how the Fair Trade premium money should be spent.

LEFT
PLUCKING LEAVES ON A PLANTATION THAT IS INVOLVED IN THE FAIR TRADE SCHEME.

Decaffeinated tea

For drinkers who cannot consume caffeine, decaffeinated teas are available, but tend to lack flavour and body. Three solvents are available to manufacturers of decaffeinated teas – carbon dioxide which in small quantities is harmless but involves expensive equipment; ethyl acetate which is expensive; and methylene chloride which is now banned in the United States and Germany. A good alternative to decaffeinated tea is to drink green teas and oolongs, which contain very little caffeine. They also taste a great deal better than the decaffeinated version.

Instant tea

Instant tea is made by brewing tea in large quantities in a special plant, separating the infusion from the leaf, concentrating the tea solids from the infusion, then drying the concentrated tea solids by freezing them or by spray-drying them through a hot air chamber. The tea is sold in jars in powder or granule form. It is hard to imagine a time when instant tea will replace tea bags or loose leaf tea. After all, spooning some into a cup and adding boiling water is no easier than opening a caddy, spooning a few leaves into a pot and pouring on boiling water.

LEFT

IN TURKEY, TEA IS ALWAYS AT THE CENTRE OF BUSINESS AND SOCIAL LIFE.

OPPOSITE

AT A TEA PLANTATION IN AZERBAIJAN, THE DIRECTORS OF THE COMPANY TAKE TEA.

TEA CEREMONIES

OPPOSITE
LATE NINETEENTH-CENTURY PRINT OF THE JAPANESE TEA CEREMONY.

Every tea-drinking nation around the world has its own way of brewing and serving the beverage. In Tibet, green brick tea is churned with yak's milk, salt and butter and served in bowls; in Russia, where the samovar still takes pride of place in many homes, a strong black concentrate of tea is brewed in a pot, then poured into cups and diluted with boiling water; the British still serve their traditional afternoon tea; while the historic rituals of China and Japan still play a part in the everyday life of those countries.

BELOW
SINCE THE 1820s, AFTERNOON TEA HAS HELD A SPECIAL PLACE IN BRITISH SOCIAL LIFE.

Brewing a pot of tea

Regardless of the type of pot or the tea you use, there are certain rules which must be followed to achieve the best possible infusion:

❖ always use cold water that has been freshly drawn from a tap or filter jug (tea needs oxygen to infuse properly; stale water that has already been boiled and left to cool will give a flat taste to the tea);

❖ use tea which has been stored carefully in an air-tight container that has been kept in a cool, dry place;

❖ choose a teapot or other brewing vessel that is the right size for the number of cups you wish to make;

❖ warm the pot with a small amount of almost-boiling water. Swill it around, then tip the water away, leaving a clean, hot, empty pot;

❖ measure the tea carefully into the pot – the general rule is one rounded teaspoon (2.5 grams), or one tea bag, per cup, although this will vary according to personal taste and the type of tea.

FOR GREEN TEA:
Bring the water to the boil and then leave it to cool slightly before pouring it on to the leaves. Green tea tastes bitter if brewed with boiling water: Different types of green tea need different temperatures;

FOR BLACK AND OOLONG TEA:
When the water is boiling, take the teapot to the kettle or pan and pour the boiling water on to the leaves. Put the lid on the pot and leave to infuse for the amount of time indicated on the packet; the general rule is that the smaller the pieces of leaf, the

quicker the tea will brew, and vice versa. Oolongs take the longest.

It is important to bear in mind that hot water from a jug or thermos is not hot enough for brewing black or oolong tea. The way in which many hotels and tea rooms around the world serve tea bags and hot (not boiling) water does both the tea and their customers a great disservice.

If a cup or a mug of tea is brewed using a tea bag, never pour the milk into the brew until the tea has finished brewing. The leaves need boiling water and oxygen to brew properly and the addition of milk to the bottom of the cup with the tea bag will prevent this.

Traditional teapots

Tea can be brewed successfully in pots of just about any shape, made of any material, except aluminium or enamel. Most people today use porcelain, stoneware, pottery or glass.

Look out for certain features when choosing new or antique teapots:

BELOW (LEFT TO RIGHT)
EIGHTEENTH-CENTURY LENZBERG FAIENCE TEAPOT IMITATING THE FANCIFUL DECORATION OF CHINESE TEA WARES; STAFFORDSHIRE SALT GLAZE TEAPOT DECORATED WITH VINE LEAVES AND GRAPES; MEISSEN IMARI TEAPOT PAINTED WITH FLOWERS AND GRASSES; MEISSEN CHINOISERIE-STYLE TEAPOT DECORATED WITH CHINESE FIGURES TAKING TEA.

❖ choose a pot that has a lid with a hole in it so that when you pour, air taken into the pot prevents the tea from dribbling down the spout;

❖ there should be a lug on the lid to stop it from falling out of the pot as you pour;

❖ the best shape for a spout that does not dribble is completely straight and narrower at the pouring end than at the teapot end;

❖ a strainer built into the base of the spout will help to catch some of the leaves as you pour;

❖ make sure the handle allows you enough room to pick up the pot without burning your fingers against its side.

When you brew loose leaf tea in a teapot, remember that after a certain time the tea will begin to taste bitter or stewed. It is therefore better to separate leaves from boiling water by straining all the tea into cups ready for drinking or, if this is not possible, strain the brewed tea into another warmed teapot and keep the pot warm under a tea cosy. (If you are using tea bags, lift them out as soon as the tea has brewed.)

RIGHT

SUMMER AFTERNOON

TEA IN THE GARDEN.

Infuser pots

One-size-fits-all infusers made of muslin, metal or porcelain are a great help in successful brewing, but you can also buy pots with built-in infusers that make things even easier and neater. Simply place your loose leaf tea in the infuser which sits inside the pot and then lift it out when the infusion has reached the required strength. This method avoids over-brewing, the leaves are easy to dispose of,

the infuser always gives the leaves enough room to swell and release their flavours, and there is no mess.

Covered infuser mugs work on exactly the same principle as infuser pots. Even if you're not really a mug person (and I'm not), these are very useful for brewing a quick cuppa with good-quality, loose leaf tea – they are the tea connoisseur's answer to the convenience of the tea bag.

Plunger pots work on the same principle as cafetières. They allow the leaf to be separated from the water at the crucial moment when the tea has reached its ideal strength.

ABOVE

SMALL ONE-CUP INFUSER SUITABLE FOR BREWING SMALL LEAF TEA.

RIGHT

GLASS PLUNGER POT BY BODUM.

Serving black tea

When serving tea in the traditional Western style, the pot should always be presented on a tea trolley or table with the following:

❖ a tea strainer, if loose leaf tea is being brewed in the pot and not inside an infuser;

❖ a jug of hot water for adding to either the pot or cups so that individual drinkers can adjust the strength of the tea to suit their taste;

❖ a jug of full fat or semi-skimmed milk when appropriate (flavoured, green, oolong and lighter black teas are better taken without milk);

❖ slices of lemon, if required;

❖ a bowl of sugar, if required;

❖ a cup, saucer and teaspoon for each person.

Milk should be poured into the cup first. There are two reasons for this. The historical explanation dates back to the days when tea first arrived by ship in Europe. Chinese porcelain wares also arrived as part of the same cargoes. Europeans had never seen porcelain before and were afraid that boiling tea would shatter the beautiful translucent bowls. So, apparently, a little cold milk was poured into the bowl first to reduce the temperature of the tea and therefore protect the china. The scientific reason is that if milk is poured into boiling hot tea, there is a risk that the tiny fat globules in the milk may be cooked or caramelized and this will alter the flavour of the tea.

British afternoon tea

Traditionally served in the drawing room or garden at 4 p.m., a full afternoon tea in Britain always includes a spread of food as well as the beverage.

Guests are seated in armchairs and sofas and small tables are arranged so that each person has somewhere to place plates and cups and saucers. The host or hostess gives each person a plate, a small napkin and a knife or pastry fork depending on what sort of foods are to be served. He or she then pours cups of tea for the guests and hands them round. Food is then offered, but there is no obligation to eat any or all of the food. Guests may have as much or as little as they wish. A full afternoon tea usually consists of neat sandwiches with the crusts cut off, scones with jams and clotted cream, and a selection of cakes and pastries. Afternoon tea usually lasts for about one and a half to two hours.

Brewing green tea

THE CHINESE WAY

The Chinese brew their green teas either in a straight-sided glass or in a covered cup called a *guywan* or a *zhong*, which has a cup, saucer and lid and serves as both individual teapot and drinking vessel.

The required amount of leaf is placed in the bottom of the glass or cup and water that has boiled and then been allowed to cool slightly is poured on to the leaves to approximately four-fifths fill the glass or cup. If a zhong is being used, the lid is then placed on top and the leaves are allowed to unfurl and infuse. When ready, the three parts of the zhong are picked up, held by the saucer and lid so that fingers do not suffer from the heat of the cup, and the lid is used with extremely dextrous movements of the hands to act as a strainer and hold back the leaves in the cup while the liquor is sipped.

When the tea is prepared in a glass, an added pleasure comes from watching the movements of the buds and leaves as they absorb water and dance elegantly in the liquid, rising and sinking, swirling and twisting. More water can be added several times. The Chinese always say that the second infusion is the best, the third is the second best, the first is the third best and the fourth is the fourth best.

OVERLEAF

IN THE EARLY DAYS OF AFTERNOON TEA, ONLY BREAD AND BUTTER WERE SERVED. TODAY'S TEAS INCLUDE SANDWICHES, SCONES AND PASTRIES.

THE JAPANESE WAY

❖ Fill the kettle with freshly drawn cold water and bring to the boil. Set out a small teapot and a bowl or small cup for each person. Fill each bowl or cup with boiling water. Leave the water sitting in the bowls. This allows the boiled water to cool down to the right temperature for brewing the tea.

❖ Warm the pot with hot water, then tip the water away. Measure the tea carefully into the pot allowing approximately 2–2.5 grams per person.

❖ Pour the water from the bowls or cups into the teapot, replace the lid and allow the tea to brew for the correct number of minutes – for ordinary Sencha, allow one minute; for high-quality Sencha, ordinary Gyokuro and high-quality Gyokuro, allow two and a half minutes.

❖ Serve the tea in the bowls or cups, pouring just a little into each in turn until all the tea is served. This ensures that each cup contains an infusion of equal strength.

Brewing and serving a pot of tea is always a calming, sociable occasion, but the ritual of the Japanese ceremony is based on Zen Buddhism and involves much more than simply drinking tea. Every piece of equipment, every flower and wall-hanging, each bowl, bamboo whisk, water ladle and measuring spoon, even the colour of the kimono chosen by the hostess, have significance and play their part in the complex ceremony.

Chanoyu can last for up to four hours. After a traditional Japanese meal has been served, the ritual begins: the guests, seated on *tatami* mats on the floor, watch as the hostess lights the fire and brews the tea with precisely choreographed movements of the hands and body. Slowly and methodically, she handles all the utensils. First, she serves each visitor a bowl of thick whipped tea, which is made by whisking powdered green tea into boiled water. All the guests accept little sweetmeats made from bean curd and sugar to eat with their tea. Finally, the hostess offers each guest a second bowl of tea – this time, it is a thin green tea. Again, she offers more cakes and sweets as accompaniments. Then, after exchanging bows with the hostess, the guests leave.

5

TEA DRINKS AND RECIPES

Tea can be far more than just an amber liquid sipped from a cup. Both the leaves and the infusion can be used as a versatile ingredient in cooking and in preparing different beverages and cocktails. Now that we know that tea is so good for us, we should be adding more of it to our diet in as many different ways as possible.

Drinks made with black tea

Indian chai

Put 4–5 rounded teaspoons of black tea leaves in a saucepan and add 500ml of boiling water. Place the pan on the stove and add 500ml of fresh or condensed milk. Add sugar to taste, 1 teaspoon of cardamom seeds and 2 sticks of cinnamon. Simmer gently to allow the spices to infuse into the liquid, then strain into cups and serve hot.

Spiced tea

In a saucepan, warm 2–3 tablespoons of honey, 5–6 cloves, 1 stick of cinnamon and 1 cup of freshly strained orange juice. Add 4–5 rounded teaspoons of black tea leaves (use an Assam or an English Breakfast blend) and 1 litre of boiling water. Cover the pan, remove from the heat and leave to infuse for 4–5 minutes. Strain into cups or glasses.

Mint tea

Use a fairly strong black tea such as Assam, English Breakfast, Irish Breakfast or Kenya. Brew the leaves in the usual way in a teapot then add a few fresh, lightly bruised mint leaves to the pot and allow to infuse.

Iced tea

The best teas to use for iced tea are Ceylon and Keemun because they do not go cloudy when left to stand. Make a pot of tea using 1–2 more spoonfuls of leaf than usual and leave to infuse to the required strength. Strain into a jug and add 1 tablespoon of caster sugar or sugar syrup. Leave to cool. To serve, fill glasses with ice cubes or crushed ice, add a slice of orange or lemon and a sprig of fresh mint leaves, then pour on the tea.

Tea punch

Mix together 500ml of cold Ceylon tea, 150ml of brandy and 200g of caster sugar or honey. Chill, then add a bottle of chilled dry white wine and 1 litre of lemonade. Stir well, then pour over ice and garnish each glass with a fresh strawberry and a sprig of borage or mint.

Drinks made with green tea

Vanilla iced green tea

Brew 4 rounded teaspoons of Sencha in 1 litre of hot water and allow to infuse for 1–2 minutes. Strain into a jug and add 1 tablespoon of freshly squeezed lemon juice and 1 tablespoon of honey. Stir well and chill. To serve, use a conical wine glass for each person and place a scoop of vanilla ice-cream in each glass. Pour over the chilled green tea.

Matcha milk tea

For one serving: measure half a teaspoon of Matcha powdered tea into a bowl and add about 60ml of hot milk (normally Matcha would be made with hot water). Add sugar or honey to taste.

The Japanese sometimes also add a scoop of vanilla ice-cream to a bowl of Matcha that has been made with water rather than milk. Measure half a teaspoon of Matcha into a bowl, pour on about 60ml of hot water (not boiling) and whisk until thick and frothy. Scoop some vanilla ice-cream into the bowl and eat with a spoon.

Green tea punch

Put 4 rounded teaspoons of Bancha or Houjicha in a warmed pot and add 1 litre of water that has been boiled and allowed to cool slightly. Leave to infuse for 1–2 minutes, then strain into a jug. While the tea is still hot add 1–2 tablespoons of brandy or rum and 2 tablespoons of honey, or to taste. Serve in tall glasses or cups, and add a slice of orange or lemon.

OPPOSITE

DIFFERENT VARIETIES OF TEA MAKE THE IDEAL BASE FOR PUNCHES AND COCKTAILS.

Eating tea

Green tea lends itself to cookery more than black tea. In Japan, it is quite common to see people walking down the street eating green tea flavoured ice-creams, and for tea leaves to be added to rice, noodles, stews, sauces, tempura batters, pastries, sweets and cakes. Infused black tea makes an excellent marinade for meats such as chicken, gives wonderful flavour to foods when added to water used for steaming fish or vegetables, and beautifully plumps up dried fruits such as raisins, dried apricots and prunes that are to be used in cakes or puddings. Lighter black teas, flavoured teas and green teas all make excellent sorbets.

Tea sorbet

(Try this also with other flavoured teas such as mango, strawberry or vanilla.)

> 570ml water
>
> 175g caster sugar
>
> Freshly squeezed juice and strips of rind from 2 lemons
>
> 2 tablespoons Earl Grey tea leaves
>
> 1 egg white

Put the water, sugar, lemon juice and rind into a pan, bring to the boil and allow to boil for 3–4 minutes. Add the tea leaves, take the pan off the heat, cover and leave until cold.

Strain the tea into a freezer-proof bowl or box, cover and place in the freezer until half frozen. Whisk the egg white until stiff then fold into the mixture. Freeze again until solid.

Arrange in glass dessert dishes and garnish with a single mint leaf, and a few raspberries or strawberries that have been carefully fanned. Serve as a palate cleanser between the savoury courses of a main meal.

Tea as a marinade for chicken

Gyokuro has a sweetness which works very well in marinades for meats.

> 1 teaspoon Gyokuro leaves (or good-quality Sencha)
>
> 2–3 tablespoons soy sauce
>
> 2–3 cloves garlic, crushed
>
> 1–2 tablespoons freshly squeezed lemon juice
>
> 1 tablespoon honey
>
> 2–3 tablespoons sunflower oil

Mix all the ingredients together. Add the chicken in chunks or strips and spoon the marinade over. Cover and chill in the fridge for up to 10 hours. Lift the chicken out of the marinade and remove the bits of tea and garlic. Strain the marinade into a bowl. Grill or stir-fry the chicken, brushing from time to time with the strained marinade. Serve with salad or as a sandwich filling.

Other marinades

❖ Add half a cup of liquor brewed from Lapsang Souchong or Darjeeling leaves to marinades for chicken or turkey.

❖ Marinate cubes of lamb for kebabs in a preparation of red wine, Earl Grey tea liquor, oil, vinegar, cumin, fresh thyme, onion, salt and pepper.

❖ Mix half a cup of infusion from Earl Grey leaves into marinades for pork satay or barbecued pork chops.

❖ Add a little green jasmine or rose pouchong tea to the syrup for fresh fruit salads.

❖ Soak sultanas, raisins and currants in cold tea before mixing into tea breads, fruit cakes or scones.

❖ Soak dried mushrooms in a very, very light infusion of Lapsang Souchong before cooking.

Steaming, baking and grilling fish

❖ When cooking fish in a closed fish steamer, add a sprinkling of Gyokuro, Sencha or China oolong to the water.

❖ When baking fish in a covered dish in the oven, add a little liquor infused from Gyokuro, Sencha or China oolong to the juices around the fish.

❖ When grilling fish, add a fine sprinkling of green tea leaves that have been pulverized in a blender.

❖ When grilling kippers or other smoked fish, dip each fillet or fish into a bowl of liquor infused from Lapsang Souchong before placing in the grill pan.

Other ideas

❖ Add 1–2 teaspoons of infused Gyokuro leaves to vegetable soups and stews.

❖ Add a little jasmine, Earl Grey or Darjeeling to the water used for boiling a whole chicken, a ham or a joint of bacon.

❖ Add a pinch of chopped green tea leaves to the water used to boil rice, noodles or pasta.

❖ Dry-roast 1 tablespoon of green tea leaves in a hot dry pan, crumble and use to sprinkle over vegetables or other dishes as a garnish.

❖ Sprinkle some Matcha powdered green tea over ice-creams.

❖ When making compotes of dried winter fruits such as apricots, prunes and dried peaches, add a light infusion of Earl Grey, Ceylon or Darjeeling tea to the juice with honey and spices.

Don't be afraid to experiment with your own ideas. Think of tea as a herb and use it instead of other more traditional herbs.

LEFT

OOLONGS AND GREEN TEAS ADD A DELICIOUS AND UNUSUAL FLAVOUR TO STEAMED FISH.

HERBAL AND FRUIT INFUSIONS

OPPOSITE
**A GLASS OF MINT
TEA AS SERVED
IN MOROCCO.**

If it were not for a basic human desire to harness Nature's gifts for our own benefit, the refreshing and recuperative properties of the tea plant would never have been discovered. And by the same tasting and testing that allowed Shennong to discover the remedial benefits of tea, many other plants have also, over the centuries, been found to restore health, heal cuts and bruises and cure both major and minor ailments.

RIGHT
**HERBAL INFUSION
FLAVOURED WITH A
SLICE OF FRESH LEMON
AND A LITTLE HONEY.**

The difference between the hundreds of teas available and other herbal infusions is that all teas are made from *Camellia sinensis*. Herbals, fruit infusions and tisanes are not. They are made from various parts of other plants which have their own characteristics, flavours and medicinal values. Preparations are usually taken as tonic drinks, made by infusing the plant's fresh or dried leaves, fruits, flowers, stems, roots, bark, seeds or seed cases. Alternatively, these parts of the plant are boiled, or steeped in alcohol or other liquids to make potions and medicines, or concentrated and used in ointments. They are sometimes used alone or blended together to give a palatable flavour and the correct medicinal balance.

Some plants are poisonous, so it is wise to experiment only with those that we know do not harm or upset the body. To gather and prepare your own herbs at home, simply pick the plants when fresh and allow to dry in a warm, airy place. Then, store them carefully away from humidity and strong smells which may be absorbed and unbalance the true flavours. Many herbs can be successfully stored in air-tight bags or containers in the freezer.

It has to be said that dried whole stems and flowers are more effective since they retain more of their essential oils than small pieces that have been cut or rubbed. But if it is more convenient, you can brew your favourite infusion using one of the many varieties of bagged herbs now available from tea and health companies. They look like tea bags and should be treated with the same respect and stored carefully so that they keep their flavour and aroma.

Some herbs and fruits are bagged individually, such as camomile, fennel and peppermint. However, blends tend to offer more pleasant flavours and more than just one health benefit. Try, for example, orange peel, blackberry, rosehips, cinnamon and hibiscus flowers – a mixture that is high in vitamin C, helps to clear the digestive system of toxins and makes a refreshing spicy cup. Or drink a blend of ginseng and peppermint which helps restore energy, combat stress and soothe the digestion. There are endless possibilities to choose from – it is simply a question of tasting and deciding which combinations please you the best.

To brew, place one teaspoonful of the herb or one bag per cup into a pot (the amount will depend on personal taste and the individual herb used). To make disposal of the herb easy after brewing, use an infuser inside a pot. Whatever you use, make sure that there is plenty of space for the dried plant parts to absorb water, unfurl and release their flavours and goodness into the water.

Pour on boiling water and leave to infuse for about five minutes. Strain off the liquor, or lift the infuser from the pot, and your herbal brew is ready to drink. Like many real teas, infusions should be drunk without milk but perhaps with the addition of honey, lemon, lime or orange zest or juice.

OPPOSITE

HOT AND ICED HERBAL AND FRUIT INFUSIONS OFFER A CAFFEINE-FREE ALTERNATIVE TO COFFEE OR TEA.

Therapeutic herbs and fruits

Aniseed: A digestive that is also thought to ease bronchial complaints.

Bergamot: Although best known as the fruit that flavours Earl Grey tea, the leaves can be infused to give a drink that is said to clear the head.

Blackberry leaves: Good for clearing toxins from the system to give a clear skin; also helpful for getting rid of headaches.

Camomile: A calming, relaxing herb that is believed to sweeten the breath, settle the stomach, calm the nerves, reduce stress and help combat insomnia.

Citrus fruits: Rich in vitamin C.

Cranberry: Aids digestion and helps prevent infection of the urinary tract by strengthening the kidneys and bladder.

Dandelion: Can lower blood pressure, help digestion and is a diuretic, so can be helpful as part of a slimming diet.

Fennel: Cleanses and calms the digestion.

Garlic: Purifies the blood and lowers cholesterol, helps the digestion and circulation, strengthens the immune system which helps keep illness at bay.

Ginger: Helps digestion, can relieve rheumatic and arthritic pain and is good for treating travel sickness.

Ginseng: Thought to boost the immune system, renew energy, help reduce the effects of ageing and make us wiser, brighter and better able to cope with stress.

Jasmine flowers: Impart a soothing aroma and flavour that help calm the nerves.

Lemon balm: Refreshing, rejuvenating and soothing.

Lemon thyme: Antiseptic; also helps calm the digestion.

Lemon verbena: Good for the digestion and very refreshing.

Lime flowers: A soporific herb, so good before bed; also helps against the early symptoms of a cold.

Maté: Grown and drunk in Brazil and Argentina, it contains caffeine so is refreshing and invigorating; also rich in vitamin C.

Pau d'arco: Comes from the bark of trees in Argentina and Brazil and has all sorts of benefits – it is rich in iron, can reduce blood pressure, helps cardiovascular problems, reduces fever, helps digestion and treats infections.

Peppermint: Sweetens the breath and calms the digestive system; also helps reduce heartburn, stomach ache and nausea.

Rooibosch: This South African plant tastes a little like tea, but does not contain caffeine. It is rich in vitamin C, mineral salts and proteins and is said to contain a high proportion of antioxidants to help the body fight free radicals.

Rosehip: Rich in vitamins C, E and K; helps ward off infections, sore throats, bladder and kidney problems and alleviates stress.

Rosemary: Good for indigestion and circulation, and promotes the growth of healthy skin and hair. (Do not use if you have high blood pressure or suffer from epilepsy.)

Sage: Good for sore throats and colds, helps reduce anxiety and depression, improves the memory, aids circulation and digestion and is thought to help us live to a ripe old age.

St John's wort: Helps reduce muscle spasms, such as period pains, lifts depression and anxiety and soothes the nerves; can be very helpful against symptoms of the menopause.

Thyme: Has antiseptic properties; can help relieve coughs and breathing problems.

Valerian: Has a tranquillizing effect which calms anxiety and nervousness; also helps reduce muscle spasms and pain. (Valerian is bitter-tasting and needs to be sweetened with honey or mixed with other sweeter herbs.)

RIGHT

THE VARIETY OF HERBAL INFUSIONS IS MYRIAD.

TEA AND HEALTH

OPPOSITE
FOR MANY PEOPLE TEA IS OFTEN THE FIRST DRINK OF THE DAY, AND SOMETIMES THE LAST.

Consumers around the world are increasingly aware of the part that diet plays in human health. What we eat and drink can greatly influence the risks of developing certain illnesses. Whereas in the past tea was enjoyed by billions of people as a refreshing beverage that did the body no harm, today it is widely accepted as actually having a positive effect on our health. Scientific evidence is emerging to suggest that the consumption of tea can protect the human body against major health problems such as cancer and thrombosis.

BELOW
FIVE CUPS A DAY KEEPS THE DOCTOR AWAY.

The Chinese first drank tea as a herbal remedy and tonic. It was referred to in the third century BC as the "elixir of life", and scholars and holy men were said to exist purely on bowls of tea. Then, when tea was first mentioned in Europe by Giambattista Ramusio in his second volume of traveller's tales (published in 1559), he wrote of the herb Cha Catai which he said the people in the Chinese province of Szechwan infused in boiling water as a cure for stomach aches and gout. Likewise, Thomas Garraway, London's first merchant to make a business from selling leaf tea, advertised it as a cure-all that was effective against dropsy, scurvy, skin problems, loss of memory, headaches, sleepiness, sleeplessness and much more.

In more recent times, green tea has been recognized for many years as possessing properties that are beneficial to health. Worldwide scientific research is now proving that black tea also has the ability to help digestion, fight bacteria in the digestive system, help reduce tooth plaque and prevent tooth decay, guard against certain forms of cancer, lower cholesterol, and generally promote health and long life. As well as the fluoride which protects the teeth, and various trace elements such as potassium, manganese, vitamins A, B1 and B2, tea has three main constituents – essential oils, caffeine and polyphenols.

The essential oils give tea its flavour and aroma and help break down fats in the blood. Caffeine acts as a mild stimulant so that, about 15–20 minutes after drinking a cup of tea, the drinker feels refreshed, revitalized, better able to concentrate and more alert. The caffeine also helps speed up the metabolism, activate the digestive system and help rid the body of toxins. It also stimulates the circulation and helps to keep the walls of the blood vessels and the heart tissue soft and healthy.

RIGHT

COLD TEA BAGS ARE SAID TO BE GOOD FOR REFRESHING TIRED OR PUFFY EYES.

However, the most important of tea's ingredients for health are the polyphenols (also known as flavonoids). Polyphenols act as antioxidants that help slow down or prevent the effects of free radicals, the oxidants that cause cell damage and premature ageing. We can't stop the oxidation process – it goes on simply as part of being alive – and we are exposed to more oxidants on a daily basis in the form of sunlight, cigarette smoke and industrial pollution in the air. But we can protect ourselves to some extent by using sun block creams, by avoiding polluted atmospheres and by eating foods and drinking beverages that contain plenty of antioxidants (for example, fruit and vegetables and red wine). The damage caused by oxidants can lead to cancers or heart and circulatory diseases, and scientists are now proving that the risk of these illnesses can be reduced by drinking tea.

In the case of mouth, lung, colon, digestive, skin, breast and prostate cancers, the antioxidants in tea appear to reduce the size and occurrence of tumours, or prevent the early indications of possible cancers from developing into tumours.

Research has also shown that the polyphenols in tea have two effects which can help reduce heart disease and arterial problems. They help reduce the absorption of fat into the blood stream and therefore help reduce cholesterol. And they help prevent the oxidation process that causes a build-up of fatty tissue in the blood vessels. It has even been shown in research that the antioxidants in tea have a more beneficial effect against this furring-up of the arteries than many fruit and vegetables whose antioxidant vitamin content has been recognized for some time. Since blockages of the arteries can lead to stroke, thrombosis and heart attack, healthier arteries mean a more efficient circulation and a generally healthier body.

Tea's antioxidant effects are also thought to be powerful against diabetes, rheumatoid arthritis, cataracts and ageing. And since tea is now recognized as containing powerful antioxidants, it is hardly surprising that manufacturers of cosmetics and skin care products are now including tea as an ingredient in sun blocks, face masks, moisturizers, cleansers, skin tonics, hair conditioners, anti-wrinkle creams, anti-cellulite creams and bath oils.

In the past, old-fashioned health tips often included suggestions such as using cold, used tea bags to refresh tired eyes, rinsing troublesome skin with cold tea, reducing the redness and discomfort of sunburned skin with a tea solution, or soothing tired feet with a foot bath made with tea. It is always fascinating that folk cures and housewives tales so often turn out years or centuries later to be absolutely correct. Now, one well-known cosmetic company advertises some of its products with the explanation that "it has been found that one of the two major pharmacologically active groups of chemicals in green tea, the polyphenols, are powerful antioxidants more than 20 times the strength of vitamin E".

In the light of all this good news, let the last word go to the Japanese Buddhist monk Eisai who was responsible for introducing tea cultivation to Japan, and who wrote in 1211, "Tea is a miraculous medicine for the maintenance of health. Tea has extraordinary power to prolong life. Anywhere a person cultivates tea, long life will follow."

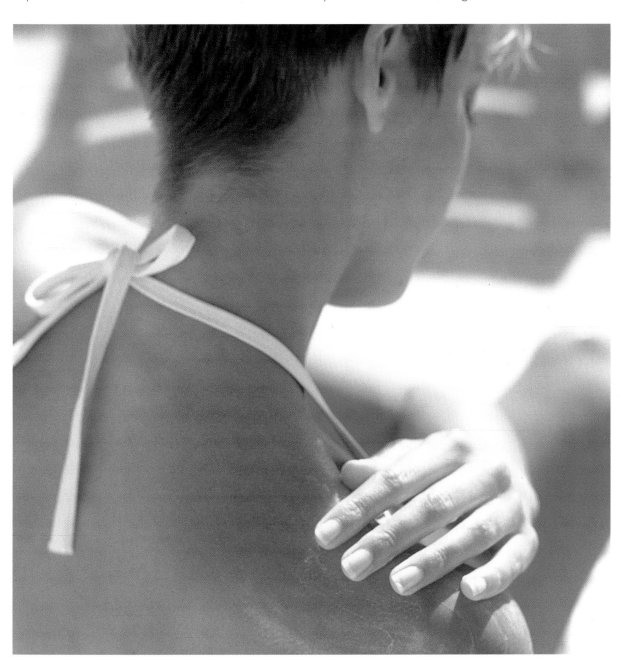

LEFT

TODAY'S SUN BLOCKS AND SKIN PROTECTION CREAMS OFTEN CONTAIN ANTI-OXIDANT TEA.

GLOSSARY

Antioxidants: Substances that help combat the oxidation of body cells that can lead to cancer; in tea these include vitamin C and polyphenols.

Bergamot: The "Chinese orange", a small pear-shaped citrus fruit, native to China and today cultivated in Italy; its essential oils are used to flavour Earl Grey tea.

Bodhidharma: Buddhist monk who founded the Zen Buddhist sect and is said to have discovered tea's refreshing qualities when it helped him stay awake during a seven-year meditation.

Boston Tea Party: When George III of Britain imposed import tea taxes on the American colonies, North Americans refused to allow shiploads of tea to be unloaded in ports on the American coast. In Boston, men dressed as native Americans stormed three ships on the night of December 16, 1773 and tipped their entire cargoes of tea into the harbour.

Caddy: From the Malay word "kati", meaning a measure of about 1⅓lb; the common name in English for a tea container since the 1780s. Before then, tea containers were known as tea jars or tea chests.

Camellia sinensis: The tea plant, also known as *thea sinensis*. The tea industry recognizes three subspecies – *Camellia sinensis sinensis*, *Camellia sinensis assamica*, and *Camellia sinensis* subspecies *Lasiocalyx*.

Cha: The Mandarin Chinese word for tea which became "chai" in India and Russia, and "cha" in Portuguese and Japanese. The Chinese Amoy dialect word "te" was adopted by early Dutch traders and passed as "tea" to English, "thee" in Dutch and German, "te" in Italian, Spanish, Danish, Norwegian, Swedish, Hungarian and Malay, "thé" in French, "tee" in Finnish, and "tey" in Tamil.

Chanoyu: The Japanese Tea Ceremony.

Clipper ships: Fast, streamlined ships that took over the transportation of tea from China to the United States and Europe in the mid-nineteenth century. The first American clipper was launched in 1845. The first British clipper, *The Stornoway*, was launched in 1850. The average clipper speed was 18 knots.

Clonal tea: Tea plants grown by cloning from leaves taken from a carefully selected mother plant in order to improve quality, yield, disease resistance, etc.

Clotted cream: A thick cream made from milk with a high fat content (at least 56 per cent fat); traditionally served with scones and jam.

Compressed tea: Green, oolong or black tea that has been pressed into cakes or blocks.

CTC manufacture: The cut, tear and curl method of manufacture which chops withered leaves into very small pieces before the oxidation and firing processes. The method produces tea which brews very quickly and gives a strong coloury brew.

Cutty Sark: Clipper ship that is in dry dock at Greenwich in London. Visitors can go on board to see the cabins and the way in which tea chests were stowed during the voyage from China.

East India Company: The East India Company was chartered by Elizabeth I in 1600. It held the monopoly for trading with China until the early nineteenth century.

Eisai: Japanese monk (AD 1141–1215) who is said to have established tea cultivation in Japan and the manufacture of the type of steamed green tea that was made and drunk in China during the Sung Dynasty (AD 960–1279).

Fermentation: (more correctly known as oxidation.) After withering and rolling, tea leaves are allowed to react with oxygen, and at this stage of the manufacturing process turn from green to a coppery-brown colour.

First flush: The first new shoots that the tea plant pushes out in the spring; Darjeeling and Assam are famous for their first (and second) flush teas.

Flavanols: One kind of polyphenol; flavanols found in tea are known as "catechins".

Garraway, Thomas: First London merchant to market tea from his shop in Change Alley in the city of London. He wrote an advertising broadsheet in 1600 entitled *An Exact Description of the Growth, Qualities and Vertues of the Leaf Tea.*

Grade: After manufacture, all teas are sorted according to the different sizes of the pieces of leaf. They are divided into "leaf" grades and "broken leaf" grades.

Guywan: The Mandarin Chinese name for the covered porcelain cup for brewing and drinking tea; it consists of three pieces – a saucer, a handleless cup and a lid.

Orthodox manufacture: The traditional method of manufacturing tea involving withering, rolling or twisting by hand or machine, oxidation and firing (drying).

Oxidation: The process whereby the chemicals in tea react with the air to change the leaf from green to coppery-brown and develop the recognizable tea smell and taste (*see* Fermentation).

Pekoe: From the Chinese word meaning the little white or silver hairs on the underside of some tea leaves.

Polyphenols: Compounds with two or more phenolic hydroxyl groups; one of the ingredients found in tea, and now known to act as antioxidants to help protect the body against the development of certain cancers.

Pu-erh: An area in south-west China which produces flavoursome, peppery teas rather like Assams; also the name given to earthy, twice-fermented teas that are said to have powerful medicinal properties.

Ramusio, Giambattista: Sixteenth-century traveller who wrote of tea in his *Navigatione et Viaggi* in 1559.

Second flush: The second sprouting of new shoots pushed out by the tea plant during the growing season. Darjeeling and Assam are both famous for their second flush teas.

Shennong (Shen Nung): The legendary Chinese herbalist and ruler said to have discovered the tea plant's health-giving properties and to have encouraged the Chinese people to cultivate the herb.

Single-source/single-estate tea: Tea that is produced by one plantation or garden and is not mixed or blended with any other teas.

Sullivan, Thomas: The American tea merchant said to have invented the tea bag in 1908.

Tannin: The old-fashioned name for tea polyphenols.

Tatami: The candle rush matting used on the floor of Japanese homes and tea rooms.

Thea sinensis: The scientific name for *Camellia sinensis,* the tea plant.

Whipped tea: Powdered green tea whisked into hot water with a special handmade bamboo whisk; first drunk by the Chinese during the Sung Dynasty (AD 960–1279). The practice was taken to Japan in the eighth or ninth century and is still part of the Japanese Tea Ceremony.

Zhong: Another name for the *guywan* – the porcelain covered cup used by the Chinese to brew and drink their tea.

LEFT
BREWING TEA IN ALGERIA.

INDEX

BELOW

**FRESHLY HARVESTED
TEA LEAVES PACKED
IN SACKS READY FOR
TRANSPORTATION
FROM PLANTATION
TO FACTORY.**